UNDERSTANDING
HINDUISM

BY SUSAN BRADLEY

CONTENT CONSULTANT

Abhishek Ghosh

Assistant Professor
Religious Studies and Liberal Studies
Grand Valley State University

Essential Library

An Imprint of Abdo Publishing | abdopublishing.com

UNDERSTANDING
WORLD RELIGIONS
AND BELIEFS

ABDOPUBLISHING.COM

Published by Abdo Publishing, a division of ABDO, PO Box 398166, Minneapolis, Minnesota 55439. Copyright © 2019 by Abdo Consulting Group, Inc. International copyrights reserved in all countries. No part of this book may be reproduced in any form without written permission from the publisher. Essential Library™ is a trademark and logo of Abdo Publishing.

Printed in the United States of America, North Mankato, Minnesota
032018
092018

THIS BOOK CONTAINS RECYCLED MATERIALS

Cover Photo: iStockphoto
Interior Photos: Johnny Adolphson/Shutterstock Images, 4–5; Don Despain/Alamy, 6–7; SM Rafiq/Moment/Getty Images, 12–13; Album/Florilegius/Newscom, 18; Deepak Sharma/AP Images, 20–21; Shutterstock Images, 22–23, 29, 36; Sean Heatley/Shutterstock Images, 26–27; The Print Collector/Print Collector/Hulton Archive/Getty Images, 30; iStockphoto, 32–33, 40, 90–91, 94–95; Narayan Maharjan/NurPhoto/Sipa USA/AP Images, 42–43; Sam Panthaky/AFP/Getty Images, 47; St Petersburg Times/ZumaPress/Newscom, 49; Olaf Protze/LightRocket/Getty Images, 50–51; James A. Mills/AP Images, 55; Burhaan Kinu/Hindustan Times/AP Images, 57; AP Images, 59; Niranjan Shrestha/AP Images, 60–61, 70–71; Bartosz Hadyniak/iStockphoto, 63; Aijaz Rahi/AP Images, 66–67; Rajesh Kumar Singh/AP Images, 72–73; Pete Burana/Shutterstock Images, 75; Creative Touch Imaging Ltd/ZumaPress/Newscom, 78–79; Ajit Solanki/AP Images, 80–81; Mahesh Kumar A./AP Images, 84–85; Blair Seitz/Science Source, 89; Dorann Weber/Moment Mobile/Getty Images, 98–99

Editor: Marie Pearson
Series Designer: Maggie Villaume

LIBRARY OF CONGRESS CONTROL NUMBER: 2017961409

PUBLISHER'S CATALOGING-IN-PUBLICATION DATA

Name: Bradley, Susan, author.
Title: Understanding Hinduism / by Susan Bradley.
Description: Minneapolis, Minnesota : Abdo Publishing, 2019. | Series: Understanding world religions and beliefs | Includes online resources and index.
Identifiers: ISBN 9781532114250 (lib.bdg.) | ISBN 9781532154089 (ebook)
Subjects: LCSH: Hinduism--Doctrines--Juvenile literature. | Hinduism--Customs and practices--Juvenile literature. | World religions--Juvenile literature. | Religious belief--Juvenile literature.
Classification: DDC 294.5--dc23

CONTENTS

FESTIVAL OF COLORS

Traffic was heavy on Interstate 15 south of Provo, Utah, in late March 2016. Dozens of buses joined the line of cars headed for the small city of Spanish Fork, Utah. As the parking lot of the Radha Krishna Temple filled with vehicles, early arrivers made their way to the main stage area. Dancers and musicians assembled on the platform to prepare for their performances. Meanwhile, some festivalgoers circulated through the crowd, carrying signs that read "free hugs" as others purchased packages of brightly colored powder.

Once the expected crowd of more than 35,000 had gathered, Hindu yogi Lokah Bhakti took the stage to lead the group in yoga.[1] Before long, festivalgoers became restless with anticipation. Temple president Caru Das Adhikary approached the microphone. "This will be a historic moment for us all," he said. "This is the twentieth anniversary of the Holi Festival here. Let's kick off 2016 right!"[2]

The colors used in Holi celebrations represent the colors of spring.

With that, tens of thousands of festivalgoers were invited to
throw the contents of their color packets into the air, causing
an explosive rainbow cloud of hues to settle on the crowd.
A brilliant array of colored dust covered men, women, and
children, who hugged and cheered in celebration. Onstage,
women twirled and swayed with the music. Thousands of
crowd members joyfully mimicked their movements.

Known as the "World's Happiest Transformational
Event," the annual Holi Festival of Colors in Spanish Fork
commemorates a revered story in the Hindu religion. The
spring festival of Holi is held to honor the story of Prahlada, son
of the villain Hiranyakashipu. Prahlada worshipped one of the
primary Hindu gods, Vishnu, instead of his father. To punish his
son for turning against him, Hiranyakashipu enlisted the help
of his wicked sister, Holika. Holika was known to be immune
to fire, so Hiranyakashipu lit a bonfire and had Holika sit on
the flames, clutching her nephew, Prahlada. Unexpectedly,
Prahlada emerged from the fire with no ill effects, while

HOLI CONTROVERSY

The Holi festival in Spanish Fork has been a source of controversy for devout Hindus. It is held near a university owned by the Church of Jesus Christ of Latter-Day Saints. The students from this university make up the largest percentage of attendees. Many of these students do not know the significance of the festival. One student who attended said, "To me, it was just some big party."[3] This ignorance frustrates some Hindus, who want to preserve the spiritual significance of the festival. Other Hindus aren't bothered by it, saying that even the festivals in India have largely become tourist attractions. Temple President Adhikary argues that the event encourages the most important religious ideas: loving God and loving people.

Holika was consumed by the fire. The Holi festival, named after the villainous Holika, celebrates the triumph of good over evil. The festival of colors commemorates both the colorful flames that spared Prahlada and the bright hues marking the coming of spring. Holi is also celebrated to honor the love shared by the Hindu god Krishna and the goddess Radha. Some Hindus also observe the birthday of a mystic from the early 1500s, Chaitanya, during the Holi festival.

The festival in Spanish Fork, acknowledged as the world's biggest Holi festival, is one of several Holi celebrations across the southwestern United States. The Utah location draws revelers from around the world, though many attendees are Mormons from nearby universities and towns. Adhikary says, "People don't care who you are. People don't care where you come from. They're

HOLI IN INDIA

Holi, observed annually at the time of the spring equinox, is a major festival in India. Celebratory events occur across two days. The first night is marked by the lighting of bonfires to commemorate Prahlada's miraculous protection from being burned. After a priest offers prayers, celebrants toss coconuts and various grains into the inferno. The roasted coconuts are later removed from the burning pile to be shared as a sweet reminder of evil having been overcome. On the second day, a carnival atmosphere reigns as festivalgoers gather to dust and spray each other with brightly colored powder or water. Normal social barriers and hierarchies are set aside as people of every age and class join together in jubilant celebration.

going to just love you for who you are. And what's the answer to that question of who you are? You're a spark of the divine."[4]

What Is Hinduism?

Just like other world religions, Hinduism attempts to answer the question of how humans relate to a perceived divine presence—however that presence is defined. Followers of Hinduism, known as Hindus, worship various forms of Brahman. Brahman is a singular entity without form or personal attributes. Hindus show devotion to a variety of gods, thus indirectly worshipping Brahman. In ancient writings, the number of gods was said to be in the millions. Unlike the monotheistic religions of Christianity, Judaism, and Islam, Hinduism features a complicated blend of gods, which the Western

BY THE NUMBERS

Approximately 15 percent of people worldwide identify as Hindus.[6] The nation with the greatest number and highest percentage of Hindus is India. As of 2010, 94 percent of the world's Hindus lived in India.[7] In India's 2011 census, Hindus constituted 79.8 percent of India's total population.[8] According to one projection, by the year 2050, India's Hindu population will grow to 1.3 billion.[9] Other countries with populations that are 10 percent or more Hindu include Bangladesh, Bhutan, Fiji, Guyana, Mauritius, Nepal, Qatar, Sri Lanka, Suriname, and Trinidad and Tobago. Fewer than 1 percent of US residents identify as Hindu.[10]

terms *monotheism* and *polytheism* fall short of explaining. Ramdas Lamb, professor of religion at the University of Hawaii, describes one form of Hinduism: "In Hinduism, polytheism and monotheism coexist in a relationship much like the parts of a wheel. The many deities are like the spokes, all of which emanate from the hub and each playing an important role."[5] A great number of deities, each with their own particular emphasis, such as agriculture or education, serve as practical aids in worshipping Brahman rather than being the objects of worship themselves.

Some Hindus believe that individuals can achieve oneness with the Supreme Being, Brahman, through a devotional relationship with other Hindu gods. Hinduism's primary texts were first written in the ancient Sanskrit language, and the Sanskrit expression *tat tvam asi* translates to "that you are" or "you are that." This phrase conveys that the individual self, in its most elemental form, can be one with the universe's ultimate reality.

As expressed by Adhikary, each soul contains a "spark of the divine." Hindus who follow this idea observe many worship practices designed to tap into this universal consciousness. However, Hindus generally place more value on their actions and practices than on what they believe.

Hinduism is a complex religion with many sects and approximately one billion adherents around the globe.[11] Who founded it, where did it originate, and what are the sacred texts that explain it? The answers are as complicated as the diverse array of gods who make up the pantheon of Hindu deities.

ORIGINS OF HINDUISM

To understand the origins of Hinduism, one must first understand the history of the people who settled in and near the present-day nation of India. Carbon dating of hand tools unearthed in the late 1900s suggests humans resided in what is now Pakistan, north of the current Indian border, as far back as two million years ago. Artifacts also confirm the presence of an agriculturally based civilization known as Mehrgarh in northwestern India and Pakistan as early as 8000 BCE.

In approximately 2500 BCE, an advanced, urban civilization existed alongside the Indus River in this region. These Indus Valley residents lived in Harappa, Mohenjo Daro, and other river settlements. Archaeological findings suggest a high degree of technological advancement in these communities. Cities of as many as 30,000 people were laid out in a rectangular form.[1] The cities had

Archaeologists have found evidence of pottery in Mehrgarh. People in the region still craft pottery today.

drainage systems and bathrooms with running water. Cultural artifacts have also been unearthed, including statues of what some have thought to be fertility goddesses and a stone seal with the image of a male figure seated in a yoga position. The figure has three faces and is surrounded by animals, much like later depictions of the Hindu god Shiva.

Some scholars speculate the Indus Valley civilization declined on its own. A few think invaders from the north overthrew it. Some researchers also suggest that shifting long-term weather patterns could have slowed agricultural production. Scholars speculate that the years between 1750 BCE and 1200 BCE were marked by waves of migrants arriving from the Caucasus Mountains north of what are now Turkey and Iran. The migrants, who were nomadic herders known as Aryans, brought their own cultural practices and merged them with the customs of the Indus Valley people. The Sanskrit language eventually became widely spoken in the area.

SANSKRIT REVIVAL

Sanskrit is an ancient language that has existed for approximately 4,000 years, but people are still interested in it today. Although Sanskrit is spoken by fewer than 1 percent of Indians and is primarily used by Hindu priests when performing religious rituals, some linguists and other activists seek to promote it throughout India. They wish to restore the language to its former prominence so more people can read classical Hindu literature. Sanskrit scholar Aswathanarayana Avadhani said, "Sanskrit is a language that teaches you old traditions and values. It's a language of the heart and cannot die."[2]

A New Term

Historians disagree about how much the major religion of present-day India was shaped by the Aryan migration and how much is attributable to the people who were already present in the region. The term *Hindu* derives from the Sanskrit word for the Indus River, *Sindhu*, which was changed to *Hindu* by neighboring Persians. Muslims who conquered the area in subsequent centuries referred to the people living east of the Indus River as *Hindus*, using the term not only to refer to religious orientation but to encompass race and culture as well. The non-Muslims came to embrace the term *Hindu* to differentiate themselves from their invaders. Then, in the early 1800s, the British coined the term *Hinduism* to distinguish the region's indigenous religions from Islam.

In a sense, the umbrella term *Hinduism* as a descriptor of religious customs and beliefs was created to define what the religion wasn't rather than what it was. Unlike other world religions, Hinduism has no known origins, no founder, and no central authority to guide or direct adherents. The religion encompasses not only diverse beliefs and devotional practices but also long-standing social customs, as well as believers' mind-sets and ways of life. The exceedingly wide variation in how people have practiced Hinduism through the centuries has even led some to use the word *Hinduisms*. This term reflects the great diversity—and even incompatibility—of practices loosely gathered under the umbrella of Hinduism.

VEDA ILLUMINATION

American philosopher Henry David Thoreau (1817–1862) became interested in Eastern religions after his British friend shipped him a collection of 44 books from India in 1855.[3] Thoreau, who often wrote on the spirituality of solitude, included many references to the Vedas in his essays. The Vedas' influence across time and cultures is apparent in Thoreau's writing. He once wrote, "Whenever I have read any part of the Vedas, I have felt some unearthly and unknown light illuminated me. . . . It is of all ages, climes and nationalities and is the royal road for the attainment of the Great Knowledge. When I am at it, I feel that I am under the spangled heavens of a summer night."[4]

Hinduism's origins mean that its sacred texts serve a different purpose than those of some other religions. The Middle Eastern religions of Christianity, Judaism, and Islam each base their foundational principles on their holy books—the Bible, the Hebrew scriptures, and the Koran, respectively. In contrast, Hinduism, as with other Eastern religions, grew out of an oral tradition that existed for many centuries. The Sanskrit term *sruti*, meaning "what is heard," is used to describe the sacred and timeless texts that arose from divine revelations to wise people, culminating in the written collection known as the Vedas. Most scholars believe the Vedas were written between 1500 BCE and 300 BCE. The four components of the Vedas, all in poetic form, are Rig Veda, Sama Veda, Yajur Veda, and Atharva Veda. The first three consist of hymns and chants used in worship, and the fourth has magic spells and charms. Other sacred writings were incorporated into the collection of Vedic hymns by approximately 1000 BCE. Known as the Upanishads, which translates as "sitting near devotedly," these tracts emphasize how the self can be one with Brahman. The Upanishads significantly shaped Hindu practices to the extent that they are known today as Vedanta, meaning "the conclusion of the Vedas."

The Caste System

Rigid social hierarchies have played a key role in Hinduism throughout history. They have been in place on the Indian subcontinent ever since the days of the Aryans. At that time, a social order known as *varna*, meaning "color," was established on the basis of occupation and role. At the top were priests, educators, and religious leaders, known as Brahmins, who performed the sacrificial rituals that were highly valued as a way to appease the gods. The rulers and warriors, known as Kshatriyas, kept order and protected the citizenry from outside attack. Traders and farmers, called Vaishyas, were the producer class, and Shudras were the unskilled workers. These levels were created not so much for the purpose of elevating some people at the expense of others but to ensure that all the necessary functions of society were provided for.

The first appearance of varna in sacred texts was in approximately 1200 BCE in a Sanskrit poem within the Rig Veda called the Purushasukta. As the poem goes, the cosmic being Purusha released Brahmins from his mouth, Kshatriyas from his arms, Vaishyas from his thighs, and Shudras from

his feet. Boys and men of the first three classes were said to be "twice born," which meant they experienced a second birth when they were old enough to learn some of the Vedas.

Jati Justified

Through time, these occupational levels evolved into a rigid system of social standing based on one's family of birth. It came to regulate not only occupation but also access to education, choice of marriage partners, place of residence, and many other considerations. The caste system, referred to as *jati*, which means "birth," was justified by the understanding that karma explained why someone was born to one caste or another.

Artwork from the 1800s shows a ruler from the Kshatriya class, *seated*, with a servant from the Shudra class.

Karma means that good and bad actions affect someone's future. Someone born into a low caste was assumed to have been put there because of bad deeds committed in a previous life, so such placement was seen as deserved. Marriage was allowed only within one's caste to encourage people with compatible karma histories to bear children together. It was thought to be important to preserve the existing reincarnation paths to maintain the proper social order.

As the caste system evolved, a fifth category known as "untouchables" emerged outside of the main hierarchy. People in this category were typically engaged in occupations considered ritually unclean by the higher castes. These occupations included anything involving the handling of dead bodies, such as processing animal hides, or being exposed to emissions of the

GENE POOLS

Genetic researchers have established that native Indians all trace their lineage to one of two groups: ancestral North Indians who are related to Central Asians, Middle Easterners, and Europeans; and/or aboriginal South Indians. In 2013, researchers took a closer look at the genetic makeup of various subpopulations in India. They concluded that, more than 4,000 years ago, there was intermingling of gene pools within the population that then largely ceased approximately two millennia ago. The researchers believe that the establishment of the caste system approximately 3,000 years ago and the prohibitions about marrying across class lines are largely responsible for the lack of genetic mixing in today's gene pool.

Some untouchables can only find work in undesirable, low-paying jobs, such as cleaning public toilets.

human body, such as cleaning sewers or bathrooms. At times, even doctors, who are respected for their skills, have been treated as untouchables. Many people in this class now refer to themselves as *Dalit*, which means "oppressed" in Sanskrit. These untouchables comprise nearly 20 percent of India's population today.[5] The official term used by the government of India to refer to this low-status group is *Scheduled Caste*.

For as long as the caste system has existed, there have been regional variations in the ways castes and subcastes are defined and counted. One estimate suggests there are approximately 3,000 different castes and 25,000 subcastes across India.[6] Each subcaste is constrained by social rules about jobs its members may perform, marriage partners its members may consider, and castes with whom its members may eat or drink. The system's practice has continued into the 2000s, though people within the system have repeatedly tried to reform it.

CHAPTER THREE

EVOLUTION AND COLONIALISM

Hinduism continued to evolve in the post-Vedic period, which began in the 500s BCE. Hinduism was shaped in part by the coming of Buddhism to northern India in the 400s BCE and the spread of Jainism to eastern India at about the same time. Both of these newer religions incorporated many concepts that were becoming central to Hinduism, such as a belief in reincarnation. However, they did not accept the sacredness of the Vedas or approve of the caste system that had come to characterize Hinduism.

Hinduism developed further when Hindu rulers in the Gupta dynasty promoted the worship of particular deities from approximately 320 CE to 540 CE. The period in which this empire ruled much of northern India has often been called the Golden Age of India. It was a time of peace, economic advancement, and flourishing arts.

Many temples were built during the Gupta dynasty, including the Dashavatara temple.

Also during this dynasty, cultural appreciation grew for two Sanskrit texts, the *Ramayana* and the *Mahabharata*, both of which had been written between 500 BCE and 100 BCE. These lengthy poems described adventures of great Hindu warriors. They cemented Hindus' reverence for various deities and emphasized the importance of worshipping them.

In particular, a portion of the *Mahabharata* known as the *Bhagavad Gita* rose to prominence in the 700s CE as a treasured holy writing. Its principles gained wide acceptance following the commentary of Shankara, a philosopher and theologian. The *Bhagavad Gita*, which translates from Sanskrit as "song of God," describes a conversation between Prince Arjuna and Krishna, an avatar of the god Vishnu. Krishna's replies incorporate many prior teachings from the Upanishads, including the immortality of the soul, the parallel existence of mind and body, and the importance of gaining knowledge. In the *Ramayana*, Vishnu takes the form of another avatar, Prince Rama. The influence of both these sacred writings made Vishnu even more revered.

Bhakti

Hinduism further evolved between the 500s and 800s CE with the advent of bhakti. Bhakti, meaning "devotion," was and still is based on the demonstration of intense personal emotion for one's god or gods. In general, the introduction of bhakti caused divisions within Hinduism. It encouraged sects to form to worship their own gods. On the other hand, it broke down some social barriers because expressions of bhakti were not restricted to gender or social class. People from every station in life mingled together as they went on pilgrimages to worship their favored deity. Expressions of bhakti were supported by a new collection of Sanskrit texts called Puranas, sometimes known as the fifth Veda. These stories exalted the gods and praised heroes who demonstrated faithful and passionate devotion to their deities.

At the same time that Hinduism was evolving in India in the first millennium CE, it was spreading to other parts of Asia. The earliest evidence of Hinduism in Southeast Asia comes from Borneo, where inscriptions from the late 300s CE tell of food offerings by Hindu priests. Both Hindu and Buddhist traders traveled from India to Southeast Asia. In time, large temples honoring Shiva and Vishnu were built in what is now Cambodia. Stories from the *Ramayana* and the *Mahabharata* became as familiar to many Southeast Asian Hindus as they were to native Indians.

EARLY DEITIES

In the early Vedic period, which lasted from approximately 1500 BCE to 800 BCE, many religious rituals centered around the fire god Agni. Agni was the gatekeeper to other gods, so worshippers presented their offerings to Agni with hopes that he would pass them on to the intended deity. Indra was the god of thunder and lightning and was considered the most powerful god. Soma was the plant god, so sacrifices of milk, butter, plant stalks, and other substances were offered into Agni's fire to please Soma. As the Vedic period progressed, the emphasis on ritual and sacrifice was replaced by the pursuit of philosophical concepts regarding the nature and meaning of human existence. By the end of the later Vedic period in approximately 500 BCE, Agni, Indra, Soma, and other deities had been relegated to minor roles.

Hindu religious practice in India—diverse and dynamic as it was—continued largely unhindered for centuries. It encountered the greatest challenge to its existence not because of splintering or dissension within the ranks of Hindu believers, but as a result of outside forces.

Angkor Wat in
Cambodia, built
in the 1100s CE,
originally served as
a temple to Vishnu.

Islam in India

The first major challenge to Hinduism was the Islamic conquest of northern India in 1192 CE. Muslim

armies from central Asia conquered the region, followed by Islamic preachers teaching a mystical form of Islam known as Sufi Islam. The invaders often destroyed Hindu temples and imposed Islam on those they ruled. Their reign under the Delhi Sultanate lasted until 1526, at which time they were replaced by other Muslims. These Muslims established the Mughal dynasty.

The Mughal dynasty spanned northern and central India from 1526 until 1707. For various periods of time during Mughal rule, segments of the Indian population enjoyed peace, prosperity, and a developing culture characterized by innovations in architecture and the arts. During the Mughal dynasty's development, the first Europeans to visit India arrived from Portugal in the early 1500s. They were soon joined by Dutch, Portuguese, French, and British traders, who sold European wares and purchased spices and silk from local merchants. The British East India Company, established by royal charter in 1600, enjoyed successful trading with the Mughal dynasty.

As the Mughal dynasty declined in power, civil unrest and street violence rose. The British East India Company protected its interests with soldiers. In 1757, the company defeated the nabob, an official similar to a governor, of Bengal and his French allies in the Battle of Plassey. The company, and later the British crown itself, then became firmly entrenched as the acting government in much of India.

British Rule

British colonialism in India exposed Hindus to Western religious thought for the first time, and Europeans were exposed to Hindu beliefs and cultural practices. In both cases, the responses of each

A Mughal emperor built one of the most iconic buildings in India, the Taj Mahal. The Muslim ruler built it as a tomb for his wife.

The nabob's army failed to keep its ammunition dry during a heavy rain, which allowed the British to win.

side shaped Indian history and Hinduism. The British response had two angles. The more secular response was to start schools that taught from a Western perspective. Classes were in English and were formed around Christian values. A main purpose of these schools was to train Indians to work as lower-level government officials in the growing colonial government. At the same time, Protestant British missionaries flocked to India in great numbers, objecting to many Hindu beliefs and practices as they sought to replace them with Christian doctrine and morality. Their harsh judgment of the Hindu religion caused much resentment among Indians who did not appreciate being criticized or forced to change by foreigners.

Hindus, at the same time, responded to the Westerners' hostility and their ideals by drawing together, at least to some degree, into a more cohesive religious group. Traditions, worship practices, and beliefs may have differed among the many religions on the Indian subcontinent. But the unwelcome presence of the British caused the groups to pull together against their common foe. The Hinduism label that had been coined by the British unified Indians who were eager to oppose British rule.

BUILDING AN EMPIRE

The first Europeans in India were Roman Catholic Dominican missionaries from Portugal. They settled on the west coast of India in 1510. Catholic Jesuit missionaries followed in 1540. From the earliest days of colonialism, Dutch, Portuguese, and British traders all wanted access to the rare spices and plentiful cotton, among many other riches, that could be found in India. The British East India Company formed when a group of 80 English merchants petitioned Queen Elizabeth I in 1599 to secure the right to trade with India. By the following year, the group of investors had expanded to 218, and they dominated the trade for the next 15 years.[1] What started as a commercial enterprise, however, later transformed into a major colonial power. The British fought with local rulers, expanding their political control in the region. The British eventually took control of the entire subcontinent of India.

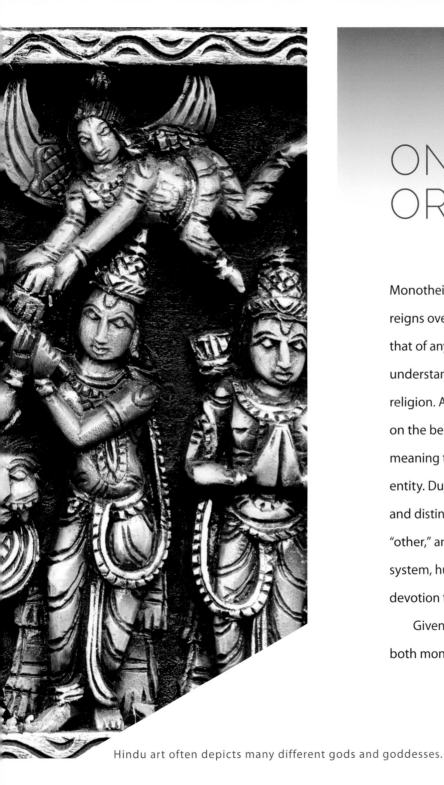

CHAPTER FOUR

ONE GOD, MANY, OR NONE?

Monotheistic religions teach that one God created the world and reigns over it and that this God's fundamental essence differs from that of any other being. Although Christianity, Judaism, and Islam understand their one true God differently, each is a monotheistic religion. A dramatically different philosophy, monism, is based on the belief that there is only one form of reality in the universe, meaning there is no distinction between gods, people, or any other entity. Dualism, in contrast, understands divine reality to be separate and distinct from the rest of the universe. There is God and there is "other," and the two are materially different. Under a dualistic belief system, humans are separate from God and therefore can express devotion to God—in whatever form they envision God to take.

Given Hinduism's origins and many centuries of evolution, both monistic and dualistic viewpoints exist under the umbrella of

Hindu art often depicts many different gods and goddesses.

WHO IS BRAHMAN?

According to the monistic philosophy of Hinduism, Brahman cannot be described in human terms. Its greatness is such that no words can define it because it encompasses all words. This concept is conveyed in one of the Upanishads as *neti-neti*, meaning, "Not this! Not that!" By stating what Brahman is not, the text means to convey that it is everything. In addition, because Brahman permeates all things and is the supreme reality, the self can then be one with it.

Hinduism. Hindus who hold a monistic viewpoint typically believe in Brahman, their name for the universe's supreme reality. Their devotional practices focus on achieving oneness with the divine presence. At the same time, they may believe in multiple gods and goddesses, none of whom is at the level of Brahman, but all of whom are worthy of devotion. Each of these gods is seen as a manifestation of Brahman but is not Brahman itself. Other Hindus do not believe in any gods at all. They follow the words of Indian activist Mohandas Gandhi: "Truth is God."[1]

The majority of Hindus practice a more dualistic expression of Hinduism. Although they often seek to be in the presence of God through worship and meditation, they do not aspire to be one with God because such oneness is unattainable. Instead, they express devotion to one or more gods while believing Brahman to be the Supreme Being.

How Many Gods?

To some degree, then, Hinduism is both monotheistic and polytheistic. Hindus believe in the concept of one Supreme Being, yet the worship of multiple god figures is an elemental part of devotional practice for most Hindus. Non-Hindus often wonder about how many deities there are. There is no definitive answer. The Rig Veda mentions 33 deities. Later, in a revered passage from the Upanishads, a wise man is asked how many gods there are. In his first reply, he says, "three hundred and three, and three thousand and three." Then, after pondering the question further, he concludes there is only one God, named Brahman, who finds expression in many god figures. Centuries later, in the Puranas, the number of gods is said to be 330 million, but many scholars say this figure was arrived at through erroneous translation of a Sanskrit work in the Rig Veda. No list of these 330 million deities has ever been produced.[2]

A central concept pertaining to Hindu deities is the Trimurti, or triumvirate. The Trimurti consists of three gods: Brahma (not to be confused with Brahman), Vishnu, and Shiva. Brahma is regarded as the creator of the universe, Vishnu is the preserver of the universe, and Shiva is the destroyer and re-creator of the universe. Carvings and images often depict a three-faced figure representing the Trimurti. Hindus also worship one or more avatars, said to be manifestations of a member of the

GANESH

One of the more beloved Hindu deities is Ganesh or Ganesha, the elephant-headed man. Ganesh is said to remove obstacles and bring success in life, so he is often worshipped before one makes a major decision. Ganesh is considered the patron, or guardian, of the arts and sciences. He is also the deity concerned with writing. According to Hindu tradition, Ganesh was the scribe for Vyasa, the wise man credited as the author of the *Mahabharata*.

Sometimes Vishnu, *left*, is depicted with the goddess Lakshmi, his wife.

Trimurti in physical form. Most avatars, including the beloved Rama and Krishna, are related to Vishnu, who is believed to have ten forms.[3] Specific avatars are believed to counteract certain kinds of evil in the world.

Sects

There are three principal sects within Hinduism based on the deity that is most revered. In Vaishnavism, followers worship Vishnu and his consort—or wife—Lakshmi. Vishnu devotees, called Vaishnavites, believe Vishnu is the All-Pervading One. He manages the world through several avatars, including Rama and Krishna. A common depiction of Vishnu shows him resting with Lakshmi on a floating serpent with a thousand heads. A lotus flower with Brahma seated on it grows from his navel, indicating that while Brahma is still acknowledged as the creator of the world, the driving force in the universe is Vishnu. Vishnu devotees see Vishnu as encompassing the entire Trimurti within himself. They also practice yoga, which combines physical poses, repetitive chanting, and meditation as a way to interact with the divine.

Shiva worshippers, called Shaivites, lean toward a more mystical religious practice encompassing yoga and, for a few, self-denial. Shiva is credited with having the power to destroy the universe an infinite number of times and then re-create it in a different form. Followers believe that faithfully dedicating bhakti to Shiva can unite them with the divine presence. Shiva's wife, Parvati, and their two sons, Ganesh and Skanda (also known as Kartikeya), are also worshipped. Shiva is most often

SIX SCHOOLS

As Hinduism has evolved in the course of more than 4,000 years, various schools of thought have arisen with respect to doctrine, holy writings, and rituals. These different ways of understanding and living out Hindu principles are grouped into philosophical systems referred to as schools. The term *astika* is used to describe the orthodox schools—that is, those that accept the Vedas as being divinely inspired and the basis for doctrine and practice. The six orthodox schools are Samkhya, Yoga, Nyaya, Vaisheshika, Mimamsa, and Vedanta. Vedanta, the most influential school, is based on understanding the Upanishads as guides for living.

depicted meditating in the Himalayas with a tiger skin wrapped around his torso. A snake encircles his neck, and a third eye on his forehead is turned inward to reflect his meditative posture. His matted hair is understood to have the Ganges River flowing through it.

The third major sect, Shaktism, is centered around worship of the Great Goddess, alternately named Devi, Mahadevi, or Shakti. Some Hindus who hold a low view of Brahma in comparison with the other members of the Trimurti view the Great Goddess as his replacement. Shaktas, or followers of the Great Goddess, revere a story from the 400s CE about Devi killing a buffalo-headed demon that even Vishnu and Shiva could not defeat. Shaktas believe the Goddess creates, keeps, and ultimately destroys the universe under her rule.

In addition to these three sects, many other sects have risen over the centuries, founded on the great admiration of various gurus (spiritual teachers) and saints. Gurus are often held up as being highly enlightened and thus are believed to have unique and direct access to God. Sometimes they have disciples who take on the gurus' spiritual power and position when they die. Saints are respected as followers who were fully devoted to their deity or deities during their lifetime.

Deity Images

Hindus make extensive use of images to facilitate deity worship. Whether at home or in the temple, worshippers revere images in the form of paintings, statues, carvings, and more. The tangible presence of the deity serves to focus worshippers' thoughts on the god's attributes, but it also serves as confirmation that the divine presence is with them. To Hindus, seeing an image or icon of a deity is as good as seeing the actual god.

Deities are often portrayed in human form with several arms, legs, or faces to represent various aspects of their character and to convey the extent of their power and skill. For example, the goddess Durga is often depicted with eight or ten arms, each one holding a weapon given to her by a god to use in battle. Some believe she protects the ten directions—the eight directions of the compass as well as up and down.

God in Nature

Nature and features of nature are highly revered as expressions of the divine presence. Mountains and rivers are historically where many sacred rites take place. Rivers are believed to be manifestations of

Shiva, Vishnu, and Brahma created Durga to destroy a demon none of them could kill.

gods and goddesses, and they are seen as places where earthly life and the divine presence intersect. Many Hindus bathe in rivers with the objective of washing away their sins, and river water is used in various purification ceremonies and sacrificial rituals. The Ganges River is regarded as the holiest river of all, and many Hindus make pilgrimages to the Ganges to bathe in its waters.

Cows are held in extremely high regard by Hindus. Cows have appeared throughout Hindu mythology. Their ability to provide milk and sustenance elevated them to their current cultural and religious status. They are viewed as maternal figures. Because of this view, they are not butchered

SACRED COWS

The penalties for harming cows have long been severe in India, but in 2017, the Indian state of Gujarat stiffened the punishment to a maximum of life in prison for slaughtering a cow. "To Indians, the cow symbolizes all other creatures," wrote Gujarat's chief minister, Vijay Rupani, on Twitter. "The cow is a symbol of the earth, the nourisher, the ever-giving, undemanding provider."[4] However, there are some legal slaughterhouses in India.

In the district of Mewat, the Cow Protection Task Force formed in 2016 to investigate the suspected sale of beef. Police, acting on rumors, raided the stands of street vendors to determine whether there was beef in the vendors' biryani, a popular local dish consisting of meat, rice, and vegetables. They collected samples of the food in plastic bags to test whether the meat was beef. The police also work closely with informants who track cow smugglers. Suspected cow smugglers are seldom given the benefit of the doubt if they are caught. Human rights activist Shabnam Hashmi said, "The hatred [for cow smugglers] has reached a level that you can even make an announcement from a temple and a crowd will go and attack."[5] However, this violent response is found only in certain parts of India.

when they no longer produce milk. Worshipping them displays respect for living things that do no harm to others, a valued principle within Hinduism.

Although gods and goddesses are at the heart of Hindu teachings, the practice of Hinduism is organized around moral laws and customs that shape Hindus' religious expression. The underlying beliefs provide a framework for how Hindus conduct their lives, and long-observed customs afford a means of keeping traditions and beliefs alive in the modern world.

KEY CONCEPTS AND CUSTOMS

In view of the many sects and belief systems within Hinduism, it is impossible to explain its many doctrines with great precision. A number of key concepts are shared by most Hindus, though they are expressed in a multitude of ways. One of these concepts is the Atman. Atman refers to the eternal individual soul. It translates from Sanskrit as "soul" or "breath." The soul goes beyond a person's physical body and is one with the universe in the past, present, and future.

Samsara, a Sanskrit word sometimes explained as "flowing around," refers to the perpetual cycle of birth, death, and rebirth. This cycle is sometimes called reincarnation. It underscores Hindus' understanding of their existence. They believe their Atman will reside in another form after their physical death, whether it be human,

Because Hindus believe people's souls live on after death, believers participate in rituals that can give deceased loved ones better lives.

FOUR STAGES OF LIFE

In classical Hinduism, four ashrama, or stages of life, were described for upper-class men. The first was the student phase, in which young men were to learn about spiritual matters and other subjects under the direction of a wise teacher. The second was the householder stage, involving marriage and raising children. In the third stage, the men were called to be forest dwellers who withdrew from society and focused on meditation and spiritual rituals. Often the men did this with their wives. In the final stage, they were to take on the role of a homeless wanderer, moving closer to the awareness of their essential natures that they had begun cultivating in the third stage. Free of all possessions except what they could carry, men in this stage were expected to focus on meditating, practicing yoga, and making holy pilgrimages. Women could also follow this path, although women typically did not take part in the fourth stage. Although these stages do not play out in these same forms in modern society, the underlying principle of life stages still resonates with many Hindus.

animal, spiritual, or even vegetable. Hindus seek to be released from samsara by reaching a state of awareness in which they embrace the oneness of all things.

Future: Karma and Moksha

The manner in which one's Atman proceeds through successive forms is based on karma. Translated from Sanskrit as "act," karma is based on the understanding that the nature and quantity of good actions and bad actions determine one's future samsara. Karma, a key aspect of Hindu philosophy, encourages believers to live a moral life. People strive to do all they can to foster good karma so as to enhance their next life. Similarly, they avoid doing negative deeds that will result in taking an undesirable form in their next existence. In a sense, karma acts as a spiritual bank account in which one's good deeds are totaled against one's bad deeds. A positive balance bodes well for a better life in the future, and a negative balance means the next incarnation, or bodily form, will be unpleasant.

FOUR AIMS OF LIFE

Hindus today seek to achieve the four aims of life. These aims summarize the way to live a balanced and productive life. *Artha* pertains to material success and social standing. Hindus are encouraged to achieve financial success and to enjoy the fruits of their labors. *Kama* involves experiencing physical pleasure. *Dharma* is achieved by fulfilling one's duty to family and society in a way suited to one's class. *Moksha*, though not widely achieved, is the ultimate goal of all Hindus.

The ultimate goal of Hindus is to achieve moksha, or release from further reincarnation. Moksha can occur only when one is free from karma, whether good or bad. Moksha is realized when one's Atman becomes aware of its essential nature, which for monistic Hindus means unity with Brahman. Dualistic Hindus seek instead to have their Atman dwell eternally with God. Different traditions emphasize different ways of achieving moksha. For example, Vaishnavites emphasize love and religious service as the best ways to pursue moksha. Hindus who are devoted to Krishna seek moksha by worshipping their deity in every aspect of life.

THREE PATHS TO MOKSHA

There are three general approaches, called margas, to spiritual liberation. They are karma-marga, emphasizing ritual practices and performing one's duties; jnana-marga, focusing on gaining knowledge through study and contemplation; and bhakti-marga, involving displays of devotion to deities through worship. The three margas are viewed as compatible and complementary, and most modern Hindus practice more than one in their pursuit of moksha. All three forms are designed to redirect one's focus on self and to increase knowledge of the divine. By focusing one's attention and great adoration on one or more deities, people fully understand the nature of reality, allowing them to escape the effects of karma and be released from samsara.

How to Live

Several concepts guide how Hindus live in pursuit of their ultimate goal of attaining unity with Brahman. Dharma concerns one's duty to uphold moral law and live a good life. Often used to mean law, duty, truth, or righteousness, dharma is a guiding principle for Hindus. It applies in a general way to every Hindu and in specific ways according to social class.

In line with their acceptance of karma as a guiding principle, many Hindus assert that what one does in life is more important than what one believes. For many practitioners of Hinduism, their religion is more about a way of life than it is about doctrine. A key component of any practicing Hindu's life is worship. Hindus go to the temple for darshan, which is a Sanskrit word meaning "to see." They believe that seeing and being seen by the deity they worship is the way to build an intimate relationship with him or her.

To honor the deities they worship, temple attendees make ritualistic offerings, often 16 in number.[1] Offerings may include items such as fruit, perfume, articles of clothing, and flowers. Worshippers may also bathe the deity's representation in scented water, milk, or other substances while chanting or speaking certain words repetitively. The Sanskrit word *puja* is used to encompass all the ways deities can be worshipped, whether in a temple or in another setting. Since deities are understood to have taken human form, worshippers seek to pay their respects in a way that activates and pleases all five senses.

Worshippers offer flowers and pour milk over a representation of Shiva.

Prayer is another way Hindus worship. Although Hindus are always free to pray for things such as a loved one's recovery from illness, the Hindu calendar denotes the dates and times when certain prayers are particularly appropriate. Those dates are determined by factors such as the month, the season, and the position of the moon and stars. Prayer rituals may include sipping and pouring water or using a special breathing technique.

Most Hindu homes contain an altar of some kind. It can be as simple as a shelf in a bedroom where small statues are kept. Or it may be as elaborate as a wooden structure with an icon inside. The altar typically faces the east, and it often includes the following items: an image of the god or goddess to be worshipped, a piece of cloth with which to cover the altar, incense or other fragrant items, oil lamps, and ceremonial dishes. Worship ceremonies involving these items may be as brief as several minutes or as lengthy as several hours. Longer ceremonies typically include an opening prayer to invite the family deity to be present, a prayer for cleansing, and perhaps a 16-step *upachara*, which is a series of offerings of items such as a sweet drink, perfume, or flowers.

Every home altar is unique. Decorations can include candles, pictures, and jewelry.

Many Hindu rituals are done to increase a person's prospects for a better life. Whether through amassing good deeds during one's lifetime or worshipping deities with devotion, the objective is always for the Atman to find a favorable home during the next incarnation. In large part, however, the course of a person's life is determined by the social class of the family into which he or she is born.

REFORMING HINDUISM

Largely in response to colonial domination, a Hindu reform movement took hold and grew during the mid-1800s. Known as the Hindu Renaissance, this movement sought to restore the former prominence of the Hindu religion in India and to address social and moral concerns. The movement also adopted elements of the 1800s European Enlightenment that supported a rational, scientific worldview.

Ram Mohan Roy is credited as the earliest and most influential reformer during this period. Born in 1772, Roy was a well-educated Brahmin (a person of the highest social class) who studied at the Muslim University at Patna. Often regarded as the father of modern India, Roy's training by Muslims gave him a strong dislike for

A statue commemorating Ram Mohan Roy stands in Bristol, United Kingdom, where he died.

worshipping images. Roy rejected traditional Hindu concepts. To Roy, the key to improving Indian society was to return Hinduism to what he saw as its rational, ethical roots.

To further his goals for reform, Roy founded a movement called Brahmo Sabha, later renamed Brahmo Samaj. Its English title was Fellowship of Believers in the One True God. Writings from the movement were influential in introducing the West to Hinduism.

Dayananda Sarasvati, a reformer born in 1824, argued that the Vedas were the sole revelation for Hindus and that Hindus should abandon worshipping icons and images. He advocated worshipping an eternal, universal god. The religious society he founded in 1875, the Arya Samaj, spoke against practices such as discrimination by social class, child marriage, and mistreatment of women. The society favored education for both boys and girls, and it founded many schools and colleges that still exist today. Arya Samaj's supporters believed that relying on the Vedas would restore India to self-government.

RATIONAL REFORMER

Ram Mohan Roy was a committed monotheist who believed in the Supreme Being that he found throughout the Vedas and the Upanishads. Roy was both a religious reformer and a social reformer. He aimed to stamp out many Hindu practices that were based on superstition, discrimination tied to social divides, and practices such as sati, the forced suicide of widows, often by burning. Roy advocated tolerance for many religions, asserting that all religions share the same purpose of worshipping the creator of the natural world.

Mystic Paramahamsa Ramakrishna, born in 1836, was known for experiencing intense, trancelike states during which he said he was communing with the goddess Kali as well as Christianity's Jesus and Islam's prophet Muhammad. He taught that there was one divine presence that people of many religions worshipped, but that no religion could tap into the totality of the divine. His primary disciple, Narendranath Datta, born in 1863, embraced Ramakrishna's universalist philosophy and asserted that recognizing the divine presence in other people was the key to social harmony. Datta, who by then had taken the name Vivekananda, addressed attendees at the 1893 World's Parliament of Religions in Chicago, Illinois, exposing many to Hinduism for the first time. He made Ramakrishna's teachings more accessible to Westerners, who valued rationality over mysticism. He endorsed the unity and value of all religions and advocated for material support for India rather than missionaries who sought to convert

TOTAL TOLERANCE

Vivekananda electrified the audience of religious leaders when he spoke at the World's Parliament of Religions in 1893. He was only 30 years old at the time. His message of tolerance and his affirmation of other religions was eagerly received by an audience that was meeting a Hindu for the first time. Vivekananda remarked, "Holiness, purity and charity are not the exclusive possessions of any church in the world, and . . . every system has produced men and women of the most exalted character. In the face of this evidence, if anybody dreams of the exclusive survival of his own religion and the destruction of the others, I pity him from the bottom of my heart."[1]

Hindus to Christianity. Vivekananda founded the Ramakrishna Mission, consisting of monks dedicated to philanthropy and the pursuit of spiritual development. Dozens of hospitals and more than 6,000 educational centers started by the Ramakrishna Mission still exist today.

The most famous Hindu reformer was Mohandas K. Gandhi, the humble leader of the 1900s. He led India toward independence from British rule. Gandhi, born in 1869 to a merchant family that worshipped Vishnu, studied law in London, England. While there, he read English translations of classical Hindu texts, including the *Bhagavad Gita*, and was also exposed to the Bible and European mystical writings. The central principle that came to direct Gandhi's life was satyagraha, meaning "grasping the truth" in Sanskrit. He believed that because each person's essence was one with the Supreme Being, there should be peace and harmony between all people. Gandhi was an outspoken advocate for social justice and nonviolent conflict resolution. Discrimination on the basis of caste has been a long-standing problem in India, particularly for those deemed untouchables. Gandhi was an early champion denouncing the demeaning treatment of untouchables in Indian society. In 1932, he went on a hunger strike to protest the British government's intention to allow untouchables to vote only in separate elections apart from the general electorate. These people would only vote for other untouchables. Gandhi thought separate elections would permanently marginalize untouchables and would make permanent the social class structure he detested. Although many credit him with promoting awareness for the plight of untouchables, some found it patronizing for him to call

Gandhi spoke against the mistreatment of untouchables.

them Harijan, meaning "children of God." Many would have preferred that he turn his attention to demolishing the caste system altogether rather than focus on the untouchables.

A contemporary of Gandhi's, Bhimrao Ramji Ambedkar, did seek to eliminate the caste system. Born in 1891 as an untouchable himself, Ambedkar overcame the discrimination he faced in India and pursued his education in England and the United States. When he returned to India, he became a fiery spokesman against the caste system, saying, "Nothing can emancipate the outcaste except the destruction of the caste system."[2] He clashed with Gandhi in 1932 over the issue of having separate elections for untouchables. In his view, voters at large would never overcome their biases enough to elect untouchables, so untouchables would never be elected. But when Gandhi, who was widely revered throughout India, was near death after six days of his hunger strike, Ambedkar settled for a guarantee of legislative seats for untouchables instead of separate elections. He feared nationwide violence against untouchables if Gandhi were to die because of the two leaders' standoff on this issue.

In part because of Gandhi's leadership in the Congress Party, India gained its independence from Britain in 1947. A Hindu extremist murdered Gandhi in 1948. Gandhi's celebrated contributions to the Indian independence movement earned him the honorary title mahatma, meaning "great-souled one."

Ambedkar also played a major role in India's new independence by helping draft the new Indian constitution in 1947. Ambedkar became the chief spokesperson advocating caste system reform. He eventually grew so frustrated about being unable to undermine the caste system that he converted to Buddhism in 1956, dying shortly thereafter of an illness. Prior to his death, he urged others to join him in abandoning Hinduism, saying, "Why do you remain in that religion which prohibits you from entering a temple . . . from drinking water from a public well? Why do you remain in that religion which insults you at every step?"[3]

Since its earliest days, Hinduism has been a complex religion that has puzzled outsiders, both in terms of doctrines and cultural practices. The religion continues to evolve even today, whether through reforms in response to outside forces such as colonialism or through natural evolution. One characteristic has set Hinduism apart from the Middle Eastern religions more commonly known in the West: its many gods. Understanding how the colorful web of deities coexists with the concept of one Supreme Being is essential to comprehending Hinduism.

Indians celebrated Ambedkar's 125th birthday anniversary on April 14, 2016.

MOHANDAS GANDHI

Mohandas Gandhi was born into a well-respected Indian family. His parents decided he needed training in the law if he was to continue the family tradition of government service. They reluctantly sent him to London when he was 19 years old. Gandhi struggled to adjust to the Western lifestyle. Coming from the small city of Rajkot, he was unaccustomed to the food, dress, and social customs in London.

Returning to Rajkot, Gandhi began his legal career. His shyness made him fairly ineffective in advocating for his clients, however, and he ran out of job prospects in India. As a result, he accepted a low-paying one-year position with an Indian firm in South Africa. While still a new resident in South Africa, a judge ordered Gandhi to remove his turban in a courtroom. Gandhi refused. Later, a coach driver tossed Gandhi out of a first-class train compartment and then beat him when Gandhi wouldn't give up his seat to a European passenger. These experiences inspired Gandhi to dedicate his life to protecting the rights of

Gandhi, *center*, faced discrimination in South Africa because of his race.

minorities and other oppressed people. He worked in South Africa for 21 years until returning to India to continue his activism. His philosophy of nonviolent civil disobedience revolutionized the way people bring change. It inspired the American civil rights protests of racial inequalities in the United States during the 1950s and 1960s.

PERSONAL DEVOTION

As with any religion, the level of devotion exhibited on a regular basis differs from one believer to the next. Many people who self-identify as Hindus engage in devotional practices only sporadically, but others center their entire lives around the worship of their deities. Each family decides how to practice its faith in a way that works for it.

Temples and Spiritual Leaders

In addition to worshipping at home on a regular basis, many Hindus worship together at their local temples. Often, temples are constructed in a manner consistent with rules specified in the Vedas, including everything from the materials statues should be made of down to the proper month, day, and time to begin construction. There are also extensive rules about how the temple should be laid out and which rooms and shrines it must have. Worship services are

Worshippers sometimes dance on special occasions, such as during Tij, when women pray for good marriages.

TEMPLE ICONS

In the temple, two types of icons are typically displayed. The first includes images of deities, often made of stone, that are permanent parts of the temple. They stay in one place. The second type includes icons known as processional images. These sculptures can be carried around during festivals and are often decorated with jewelry and fine clothing. The icons are usually made from a combination of five metals. For either type of icon, devotees gaze at the icons as part of their worship. Worshippers also seek to place themselves in the icons' line of sight. They believe that the gaze of each icon brings them blessings and the divine presence.

typically held on a daily basis at sunrise, noon, and sunset. Activities may range from singing hymns to chanting to dancing. Special services and celebrations are held on holy days that honor certain deities.

Hindus who dedicate themselves as worship leaders or teachers are highly respected by other Hindus. Priests have typically been men from the Brahmin class, but more recently, women have assumed this role as well. The priests perform temple worship services at certain times, whether or not anyone else is present to participate in them. Priests are a valuable part of the temple community. They often offer spiritual support to families.

Sadhus are nomadic holy men or women who have renounced worldly pleasures to pursue enlightenment. Hindus see them as spiritual leaders. Swamis teach and train others through both formal instruction and personal interaction. They are typically men, but women called swaminis serve

Some sadhus live in small groups. They keep few possessions.

PERSPECTIVES

"TAKE BACK YOGA"

For Hindus, the practice of yoga is a key part of spiritual well-being and connection with the divine. Hindu scholars affirm that the spiritual tradition of yoga predates Hinduism itself. Ancient Hindu texts promote yoga as a means of pursuing spiritual enlightenment. But in the contemporary Western world, yoga is seen primarily as a means of physical exercise that improves balance and strength. Its popularity is based largely on its usefulness in increasing flexibility and muscle tone, improving posture, and promoting relaxation. William Broad, a science writer for the *New York Times* who practices yoga, says, "You see a wild correlation between yoga studios and the most stressful places on the planet . . . [because] yoga works—to unplug, to relax, to help tense urbanites deal with that tension."[1]

Some Hindus object to the severing of the spiritual connection between yoga and its Hindu roots. The Hindu American Foundation launched its "Take Back Yoga" campaign in 2008 to promote a broader understanding of the meditative aspects of yoga. Sheetal Shah, senior director of the Hindu American Foundation, noted, "the holistic practice of yoga goes beyond just a couple of asanas [postures] on a mat. It's a lifestyle, and it's a philosophy."[2]

in this role, too. A person particularly skilled at leading another person toward moksha is called a guru. A guru may prescribe readings, mantras, and other spiritual disciplines to help a person along the path to oneness with God. Swamis and gurus sometimes live at ashrams, secluded areas where they can worship, meditate, and teach.

Spiritual Practices

One way Hindus connect to the spiritual world is through yoga. Yoga means "union" in Sanskrit. To Hindus, yoga is a way to bring together body, mind, and the inner self in pursuit of union with Brahman. Gurus who teach yoga are called yogis. They train people to quiet their minds so they are ready to receive divine revelation. A holistic practice of yoga for Hindus includes lifestyle considerations, mental attitudes, and personal conduct—not only the body postures for which yoga is most known. The ultimate goal is to break down any barriers between the awareness of self and the divine.

A related contemplative practice in Hinduism is meditation. As in other Eastern religions, meditation involves focusing the mind to attain greater spiritual awareness. Often, it entails repeating certain syllables or words to clear the mind of other thoughts. As with yoga, the goal of meditation is to align and unite with the universal consciousness.

Life-Stage Rituals

In addition to engaging in devotional practices, Hindus use rituals to mark one's progress through life on Earth. These begin with pregnancy, during which expectant mothers are often kept at home for part of the time to avoid evil spirits. Hindus believe the mental and emotional state

OM AND AUM

Hindus seek to be aware of the divine presence using all five senses. The sound *om*, pronounced and sometimes spelled "aum," is often used as a meditative tool. The Sanskrit vowels *A* and *U*, along with the consonant *M*, are seen as containing the sounds that make up all words, and therefore they represent the whole universe. When chanted repeatedly, om is believed to give voice to the essence of Brahman as a universal and sacred sound. In the Upanishads, aum was said to represent the four states of consciousness. *A* was for waking, *U* for dreaming, *M* for deep sleep without dreaming, and aum for oneness with Brahman. Aum is used extensively in the practice of yoga and meditation.

of the pregnant woman closely affects the well-being of the unborn child.

There are also a number of rituals related to birth and the first year of life, including a *namkaran*, a naming ceremony that happens within two weeks after birth. It is common for children to be named after one of the parents' favorite deities. Two important milestones in early childhood are shaving the child's head and piercing his or her ears. Ear piercing occurs anytime from early infancy to age three and is believed to protect the child from harmful spirits. Head shaving takes place between ages one and three to purify the child and protect him or her from evil.

Boys in the higher castes go through a "sacred thread" ceremony in their early school years. After a ceremony involving a fire sacrifice, a boy is given a thin cord to wear from his left shoulder to his right hip for the rest of his life. This cord sometimes symbolizes his connection with the sun as the

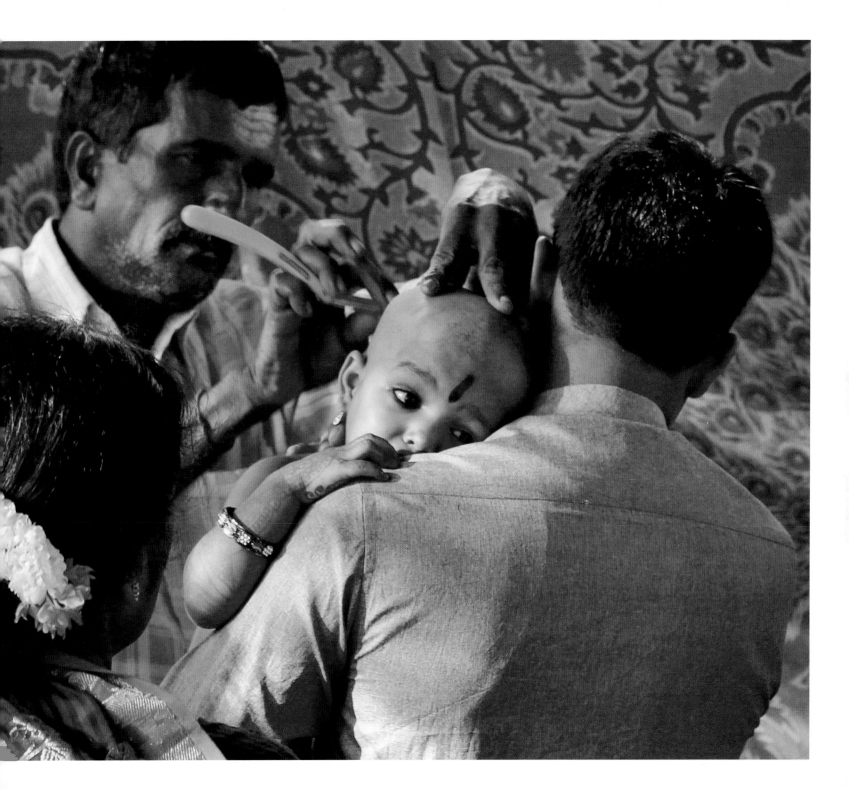

source of knowledge and wisdom. Girls go through a rite-of-passage ceremony upon having their first menstrual period.

Marriage is typically arranged by the parents of the bride and groom, though increasingly children choose their own mates with the approval of their families, or they have the right to reject choices made by their parents if they don't approve of them. In traditional society, a woman went to live with her husband's family upon marriage, but this pattern is changing as people move to cities and as more women work outside the home.

KUMBH MELA

What does it look like to assemble 120 million people in one place? Visitors to Allahabad in northern India during the 2013 Kumbh Mela festival had a chance to find out. The world's largest religious festival is held every 12 years at the junction of the Ganges and Yamuna Rivers.[3] The now-lost Saraswati River mentioned in the Rig Veda is also believed to intersect with these two rivers. The site of the ancient city of Prayag, now contained within Allahabad, is believed to be exceptionally holy because of a story in the Puranas in which several gods were fighting over a potion that guaranteed immortality. As the story goes, four drops of the potion fell to Earth in four different places, with Prayag being one of those locations. Pilgrims and holy men come to the festival from all over the world to bathe in and drink the river water, hoping to rid themselves of bad karma in pursuit of moksha.

Pilgrimage to holy sites is encouraged in Hinduism, but it is not mandatory. Although most of the designated holy sites are in India, there are sites in many other countries where Hindus reside. Many of the sites are located near rivers, as believers seek purification from their sins in the flowing water. The city of Varanasi alongside the Ganges River is one of the holiest sites, as Hindus believe that dying in Varanasi offers them immediate release from samsara. As a result, many Hindus who know they will die soon travel there or to another pilgrimage site. If they cannot go or die before they get there, they ask to have their ashes strewn in the river so their spirit can be carried into the next world.

With some exceptions, cremation is the method of disposing of a body. The eldest child of the deceased touches the fire to the deceased person's lips and then lights the pyre on fire. In traditional practice, women stay home during the cremation to sweep and purify the house after the death. The house is considered unclean for almost two weeks, during which time the immediate family offers rice balls to the deceased to help him or her find a new body to occupy in the spirit realm.

FESTIVALS AND HOLIDAYS

Given the number of sects within Hinduism and the many deities worshipped, it is not surprising that festivals abound in Hindu cultures. The Sanskrit word *ustava*, meaning "festival," encompasses the many celebrations that occur throughout a given year. Modern Hindus often refer to a calendar that shows ustavas so they can plan their personal and business activities around their devotional obligations. Because the timing of festivals is determined by solar, lunar, and astrological calendars, the date of each festival shifts from year to year.

Festivals are usually tied to the celebration of a particular deity, and many Hindus believe they can have special access to their chosen god during the deity's festival. Celebratory activities may include processionals, music, food, and ritual sacrifices. Festivals may also include devotional practices centered on prayer, meditation, or

Hindus offer gifts to the sun during a festival thanking the sun for sustaining life.

self-denial. In addition to the festivals celebrated by all Hindus, there are many regional festivals based on reverence for certain deities or natural features such as rivers and mountains. A common theme running through nearly all the festivals is good's triumph over evil.

Diwali

Diwali, known as the festival of lights, is celebrated each October or November throughout India and in other areas where Hindus live. The date of the festival is determined by the lunar calendar. Many Hindus consider it the most important holiday of the year. During the five-day celebration, people light small oil lamps or string electric lights around houses and temples. On the fourth day, celebrants dress in new clothes, sweep their homes, visit friends, entertain guests, and perform pujas to honor Lakshmi or another deity. Firecrackers are set off throughout the fourth night to celebrate the defeat of evil. Many people exchange Diwali cards to wish each other well.

DIWALI BY REGION

Although Diwali is celebrated throughout India and wherever Hindus reside, the focus of the holiday differs by region. Traditionally, and for many modern-day Hindus, the festival centers on inviting Lakshmi, the goddess of wealth, to return. In northern India, celebrants remember the story of Rama returning triumphantly to his capital city. People in eastern India celebrate the goddess Kali. In southern India, Diwali marks Krishna's defeat of the demon who ruled hell, Narakasura, and in western India, the festival honors Vishnu for sending greedy King Bali away from Earth. As the story goes, King Bali ruled the earth, skies, and underworld. When Vishnu, disguised as a dwarf, asked the king for the amount of land he could cover in three steps, Bali only reluctantly granted Vishnu's small request. Celebrating Diwali in India is not limited to Hindus, as people of other religious traditions also take part in the festivities.

Navratri

Navratri, which means "nine nights" in Sanskrit, is celebrated during the Hindu month of Ashvin, which usually aligns with September or October. The holiday centers on worshipping the goddess Devi in nine different forms, with regional variations of those forms. Worshippers wear different colors according to the day of the festival. For example, on day four, Devi is worshipped in the form of Kushmanda, who is said to have lived inside the sun. Orange clothing is worn on this day to commemorate this story. For some Hindus, the holiday period concludes on the tenth day, when statues of the goddess Durga, another manifestation of Devi, are paraded through the streets, accompanied by much singing and dancing. The traditionally clay statues are then placed in a river or ocean to dissolve.

The tenth day of Navratri, when Durga statues are immersed, is called Dasehra.

SOGGY STATUES

Traditionally, the statues used to celebrate Navratri were made of clay, but recently, other materials such as plaster of Paris and plastic have been used. When such statues are immersed in water, they often do not dissolve, creating much debris in rivers. In addition, substances applied to the statue, such as paint and decorations, are often not eco friendly. The waterways of India are already stressed and polluted, and the statues worsen their poor conditions. The Ganges River alone takes on more than 340 million gallons (1.3 billion L) of household waste every day, not to mention thousands of dead animals and a large quantity of industrial by-products.[1] Although a wide-ranging response is needed to properly address river pollution, some Indian courts have outlawed the immersion of statues as a start to cutting down on some of the debris.

Holi

Much like the Holi festival in Utah, Holi festivals all around India welcome spring with great fanfare. In the popular custom of powdering or spraying each other with bright colors, each color has a meaning. Yellow is associated with Vishnu, who is said to have made sun rays into clothing for himself. Red represents love and marriage, green signifies new life, and blue is the color used to depict Krishna.

In addition to the focus on colors, a central part of every Holi celebration is the bonfire commemorating Prahlada's fiery escape from his evil aunt, Holika. Holi is a joyous time for Hindus, and one reason it is so widely celebrated is that caste distinctions and normal rules of conduct disappear while the festivities are underway. Even police officers or public officials may be doused in colors.

A FLURRY OF FESTIVALS

Hindus observe many holidays throughout the year, often according to region or sect:

- The festival Tij (or Teej) is for women who seek a husband or wish a long life for the husband they already have. Women may sleep at the temple for a night while they hear stories about Parvati, an incarnation of Devi who sought to win a desirable husband. The date of the festival is determined by the lunar calendar, but it usually falls between July and September.

- Students and artists alike celebrate the festival of Sri Panchami (also known as Vasant Panchami) in January or February by worshipping Saraswati, the goddess of learning and fine arts. Children are sometimes taken to the temple to write their very first letters on a white wall or a slate board.

- Makar Sankranti is celebrated at the end of the harvest period. Unlike many of the holidays that are tied to the lunar calendar, Makar Sankranti occurs on the same date each year, January 14. Special sweets are prepared and shared to celebrate a successful harvest.

- Raksha Bandhan is an August festival that promotes family bonds. Sisters tie a decorative cord or bracelet around their brothers' wrists to protect the brothers from evil and to remind the brothers to love and protect their sisters.

Maha Shivaratri

A festival marking the end of winter is called Maha Shivaratri, meaning "Great Night of Shiva."

For Hindus who worship Shiva, it is the most important festival of the year. Unlike some other

Hindu holidays that are marked by joyous celebration, Maha Shivaratri is focused more on quiet

contemplation. Timed to coincide with a moonless night in February or March, Maha Shivaratri begins with an overnight period of fasting, prayer, meditation, and chanting. This concentrated time of reflection and self-denial is meant to remove the sins of the worshippers. The nighttime vigil is followed by temple worship and a simple meal to break the fast.

For Hindus, festivals and holidays serve as milestones during the year that commemorate important events or characters in their religion. Holidays bring forth a wide array of thoughts and emotions, including penitence, gratitude, joy, and love for family. For many Hindus, holidays and festivals are the centerpieces of their religious practice, rather than a focus on specific beliefs about doctrine. The practice of observing holiday traditions provides a base of constancy and familiarity for many Hindus in a rapidly changing world.

CHAPTER NINE

CHALLENGES

As Hinduism has spread around the world, several challenges have arisen that Hindus are struggling to address. One of these tensions is over the caste system. Legislation of various kinds has addressed the plight of untouchables in India. The constitution that took effect in 1950 prohibited discrimination on the basis of caste, but laws alone did not change traditions and cultural norms. Contained within the constitution were measures to address the long-running discrimination against Scheduled Tribes (indigenous minorities) and Scheduled Castes (untouchables), including quotas guaranteeing preference in hiring and education. This affirmative action program has been in force in the decades since independence, expanding in the late 1980s to include "other backward classes," meaning those of lower castes who were outside the Scheduled groups. These protections, although favored by many in principle, also have many opponents who believe the quotas deny opportunities to qualified applicants from higher castes. To give one example, in a northeastern

Some untouchables gather to protest the discrimination and violence they face.

Indian state where Scheduled groups predominate, more than 80 percent of government jobs are reserved by quota.[1] Some activists advocate for quotas on the basis of economic disadvantage rather than caste affiliation, noting that well-to-do members of lower castes sometimes enjoy an unfair advantage over more qualified but poorer members of higher castes when competing for jobs.

To be sure, progress has been made in rolling back many discriminatory practices and opening avenues of opportunity for lower castes. Disparity between castes is often most pronounced in rural areas, where one's caste often determines whom someone may associate with or whether land can be purchased. In urban areas, where caste affiliation may not be as readily known, caste distinctions tend to be downplayed. But discrimination and violence continue against the lowest castes in Indian society. As noted by Laurence Simon, director of the Center for Global Development and Sustainability, "Caste oppression is among the greatest human rights problems in the world. It manifests itself regularly through gang rapes and lynching of Dalit women. . . . Ultimately, India will have to get beyond caste as a determinant of opportunity and quality of life for millions of its citizens."[3]

Hindu Nationalism

The caste system is not the only struggle with ties to politics. Within Indian society, there is tension over the status of India's government. Some believe India should continue to be a secular democracy, even if controlled by a strong Hindu majority. Others believe it should be a Hindu state, where Hinduism drives the laws and policies. The Bharatiya Janata Party (BJP) supports Hindutva, meaning the use of Hindu values and culture in government. The BJP began its rise to prominence in the 1990s. The party wishes to end what it considers special treatment toward Muslims and low-caste Hindus. For example, Muslims

PERSPECTIVES

DEFENDING DALITS

In 2016, six assailants were filmed tying four frightened men to a truck and mercilessly beating them. The four were Dalits. They had been doing a job no one else would do: disposing of a cow carcass. The attackers wrongly assumed the men had killed the cow and decided to punish the men for it. At least one of the men was hospitalized for his injuries. In reality, the four were only removing the hide as part of their job. Agents from the higher merchant castes pay Dalits to salvage every part of a deceased cow and then sell the parts at a profit. The public outcry following this incident was huge, both among the Dalit community and in the nation at large. Dalit activist Jignesh Mevani spoke out, saying, "So [India wants] to become a leading economic power but we want to continue with such obnoxious practices. Caste should be thrown into the dustbin of history. It is nothing more than the existence of feudalism." Prime Minister Narendra Modi agreed, noting in an address to the nation, "Economic progress alone does not make a strong nation, social justice is necessary."[4]

and various castes each have different laws for things such as marriage. Until August 2017, a Muslim man was allowed to follow traditional Islamic law and divorce his wife at any time just by saying "talaq" three times. The BJP wants instead to have laws that apply to everyone equally. It also supports constructing a Hindu temple on the site where a Muslim mosque, Babri Masjid, was demolished in 1992. Some argue a Hindu shrine was on the site previously. In the decades since that event, the land has remained empty as Hindus and Muslims have fought over the issue. Thousands have died.

Another organization that strongly promotes Hindutva is the Vishwa Hindu Parishad (VHP). Founded in 1964 by religious leaders who supported Hindutva, the VHP seeks to return India to what it views as the golden age prior to Muslim conquest. To that end, it seeks further removal of Muslim shrines and mosques. It also seeks to convert Indians to Hinduism through its Ghar Wapsi ("returning home") initiative. In 2016, VHP claimed to have prevented 48,651 Hindus from adopting

YOGA FOR ALL?

The conflict over whether India should be secular or Hindu has recently arisen in the realm of public education. In 2016, it became mandatory for all students in the civic schools of Mumbai, India's largest city, to participate in a yoga sun salutation called *Surya Namaskar.* The mandate has not been well received by some Indians. Said Samajwadi Party representative Rais Shaikh, "The BJP wants to bring Hindu customs in schools, which is a secular space, and wants to force the students to do things under the pretext of culture. . . . [W]e won't let the BJP infiltrate into the minds of young children who should have the freedom to choose their religion and follow its customs."[6] Giving evidence of the great national divide on the issue of mixing religion with government, a VHP organization spokesman stated, "People who are objecting to [yoga] have no right to reside in India."[7]

a different religion and to have converted or reconverted 33,975 people to Hinduism.[5]

The struggle is likely to continue over whether India should continue to be a secular state or whether its Hindu values and traditions should formally dominate the public square. Many fear the divisiveness stoked by Hindu nationalists, which is often displayed in the mistreatment of minority groups. With recent electoral success by the BJP, including the election of Prime Minister Narendra Modi in 2014, there is concern that the religious tolerance and diversity for which Hinduism has long been known will be curtailed. Many fear that harassment, violence, and social instability could result from such a hostile civic and religious environment. Some have already speculated that the BJP forced the Christian organization Compassion International from the country. Many

Hindus feel that the presence of Christian organizations repeats the undesirable effects experienced during British colonialization.

Women's Role

A certain tension also exists in the way women are viewed in Hindu society. In one sense, women are highly regarded, as evidenced by the worship of many powerful, nurturing, and intelligent goddesses in the Hindu pantheon. A woman, Indira Gandhi, was India's national leader in the early 1980s before many Western nations elected women to leading roles. But in another sense, women have traditionally been relegated to a role of having to obey their fathers, husbands, and even sons. Only in recent decades have women—particularly those in urban areas—begun to see advances in their economic and civil rights.

One long-standing problem has concerned the issue of dowry, in which a woman's family must make a payment of money and/or goods to her new husband's family at the time of marriage. Although giving or receiving a dowry was officially outlawed by the government in 1961, the practice continues. Dowry violence has become an alarming and widespread occurrence in India. In such cases, a husband or his family members subject the wife to physical, mental, or sexual abuse to coerce her family to pay even more after the marriage. In extreme instances, women are murdered so their husbands can remarry and collect a dowry from another bride. Although a 1986 law stipulated that any death or abuse occurring within seven years of marriage would be considered dowry related, prosecution is rare.

Another issue concerns the preference of many parents for sons over daughters. Ever since the Vedic period, the preference for sons has been entrenched in Hindu tradition. In the Atharva Veda, it says "the birth of a girl, grant it elsewhere. Here, grant a son."[8] Sons are seen as bringing wealth and protection to the family. Daughters, in contrast, are often viewed as drains on families' finances since they and their dowries will move to the homes of their husbands. This problem has taken a modern manifestation in the form of sex selection before birth. In many instances, parents elect to terminate pregnancies where a girl is expected. This practice has resulted in an unbalanced ratio of the sexes. With so many more young men than young women, it can be difficult for men to find women to marry. Sikhs, Jains, and people of other religions also practice sex selection in the region.

Also of concern is the practice of sati. Sati, meaning "good woman" in Sanskrit, occurred when a widow would follow her husband's body onto the funeral pyre as a method of suicide. The first direct mention of sati comes from approximately 400 CE. The custom horrified Westerners when they first learned of it. It was never widely practiced, but the traditional belief was that in killing herself, a widow became a goddess through her devotion to her husband. However, starting in the 1100s, many cases of sati were due to people encouraging a widow to commit sati so that her husband's inheritance could be given to relatives. Sati was outlawed by the British-controlled Indian government in 1829. Occurrences of sati today, though rare, keep this issue in the public eye as a human rights concern.

Indira Gandhi fell in and out of favor with the Indian people, winning military successes but also passing several unpopular laws.

HINDUISM PRESENT AND FUTURE

Throughout its long evolution, Hinduism has been most closely associated with the nation and people of India. In a sense, it has been both a religion and a culture, even in a diverse land with more than 18 cultural regions and at least 1,000 languages.[1] The effects of Hinduism run through nearly every aspect of Indian culture and even through India's secular institutions. As the dominant worldview of the region for several millennia, Hinduism has shaped Indian culture in countless ways.

Encouraging non-Hindus to convert has never been a goal of Hinduism, largely because Hindus affirm that there are many ways to know God. They do not claim to have discovered the only way of relating to the divine, and they validate the efforts of others to seek

Hinduism has influenced cities including Varanasi, where Hindus flock for ritual baths in the Ganges River.

God in whatever form that takes. As a result, the growth and expansion of Hinduism have occurred more because believers have moved around the globe than because other people have converted. In previous centuries, this diaspora first scattered Hindus among nearby South Asian nations such as Nepal and Sri Lanka. Later, Indians fanned out to other continents to find jobs and other opportunities, including South America and eastern parts of Africa. This meant they left India and crossed the unknown *kala pani*, Sanskrit for "black waters," taking their beliefs and customs with them.

Going Global

Particularly in the last two centuries, Indian Hindus have dispersed all over the world. By 2012, Hindus lived in 101 countries.[2] Through time, they have built temples, employed Brahmins to perform sacred rituals, and organized festivals to keep their traditions alive. As Hinduism has become a global religion, many worshipping communities outside of India now include native-born Indians, as well as third- or fourth-generation citizens of many other countries where Indian Hindus have settled. The Hare Krishna movement, for example, known as ISKCON, includes Indians as well as many Westerners who desire an alternative to Middle Eastern religions. As Hinduism has spread, two opposing mind-sets have formed about what it means to be Hindu outside of India. On the one hand, some Hindus desire to foster a sense of shared traditions and beliefs that will establish Hinduism as a unified religion. On the other hand, many Hindus prefer to preserve the tolerance and wide diversity of beliefs for which Hinduism has become known. Advocates of this position believe an open understanding of Hinduism will promote peace and harmony with other religious groups. Despite Hindus holding differing views on the issue of unity versus diversity, there are not significant divisions among Hindus living outside of India. The wide availability of social media and online resources has enabled Hindus to remain connected with each other no matter where they live.

HARE KRISHNAS

The International Society of Krishna Consciousness, also known as ISKCON or Hare Krishna, originated in the 1500s in India. Its roots were in the bhakti yoga tradition, which emphasized chanting a mantra repetitively to grow in love of the divine. The movement took hold in the West after Swami Prabhupada brought it to the United States in 1965. Throughout the 1970s, orange-robed Hare Krishna devotees, also called Hare Krishnas, could be found on city street corners and in airports dancing and chanting their mantra:

Hare Krishna, Hare Krishna

Krishna Krishna, Hare Hare

Hare Rama, Hare Rama

Rama Rama, Hare Hare

The movement declined after evidence of child abuse in the sect's US and Indian boarding schools became public. Since then, ISKCON leaders have instituted measures to prevent such abuse from occurring again. In recent years, the number of Hare Krishnas has grown in the United States. ISKCON's ornate Palace of Gold in rural West Virginia has become a popular destination for worshippers and tourists alike.

In recent decades, Hindus have become more visible in the United States as their numbers have grown. As the ethnic group with the highest per capita income in the United States, Hindus have been able to construct lavish temples and otherwise cement their presence in their communities. In suburban Atlanta, Georgia, local Hindus raised more than $19 million in 2006 to construct a temple that now accommodates 6,000 worshippers.[3] In 2017, the world's largest and most expensive Hindu temple was completed in Robbinsville, New Jersey, at an estimated cost of $150 million.[4] It is one of 254 Hindu temples in the United States.[5]

As recently as the mid-1900s, many Westerners viewed Hinduism as a strange and mystical religion. In particular, the public's imagination was captured by the Beatles' fascination with Eastern meditation. The famous British band received spiritual guidance from Maharishi Mahesh Yogi, who went on to found a movement called Transcendental Meditation (TM). The Maharishi based his method on Vedic texts. The goal of TM

was, and still is, to promote world peace by teaching people to meditate. TM remains popular today, primarily as a means of stress reduction.

SHRI SWAMINARAYAN MANDIR

In August 2007, a gleaming, 27,000-square-foot (2,500 sq m) Hindu temple, called a mandir, opened near Atlanta.[6] Constructed of Turkish limestone, Italian marble, and Indian pink sandstone, the temple consists of 34,000 numbered stone pieces that were hand carved in India and shipped to the United States. Following the classical style of Indian temples, the structure is made solely of stone, with no steel used for structural support. Hundreds of volunteers helped polish stone, plant vegetation, and feed construction workers. In all, 1.3 million volunteer hours were donated to the project.[7]

Religious Reforms

With the increasing urbanization of Indian society, the face of Hinduism has changed somewhat in recent years. Many modern Hindus seek a more updated expression of their religious roots that merges their fast-paced, technological lifestyle with ancient rituals. They seek to align their faith with their personal support for women's rights, education, and philanthropy. One well-known advocate for Hindu reform was Sathya Sai Baba, who died in 2011. He challenged Hindus to maintain a balanced life by studying the ancient texts, meditating, and being attuned to the material needs of others. Under his leadership, many service organizations were established, as well as many educational institutions. Sai Baba's fame was enhanced by his mystical feats and miracle cures, making him a revered figure and a presumed representative of the divine presence.

The influence of Christian missionaries from the 1800s has also figured into recent reforms. Following the missionaries' example, many Hindu organizations have greatly expanded their involvement in social welfare and education. Recently, such involvement has been seen in the realm of environmental protection. Hindus have been pivotal in causing the Indian government to address industrial and human pollution in rivers and other locations.

Eternal Tradition

As it has for millennia, Hinduism will undoubtedly continue evolving. Hinduism remains vibrant and relevant for more than one billion people in today's modern, industrialized world.[8] Perhaps Hinduism's

MODERN MEDIA

There is nothing outdated about current methods of distributing information about Hinduism. A temple in Mumbai, India, features a live-action camera of the temple's icons, complete with sound so hymns can be heard. The website even features a donation tab so viewers can purchase puja that will be offered to the temple's deities.

Television has also been a key medium for teaching the public about Hindu lore. In 1987, weekly shows depicting stories from the *Ramayana* aired for the first time. Because many families did not own a television, groups gathered wherever they could to watch the series. Many people treated their viewing as a worship experience, bathing beforehand and adorning the television with a garland. The audience for these Sunday-morning programs was estimated at 80 million. By popular demand, the national broadcasting station went on to produce a series on the *Mahabharata*, too.

ability to adapt is founded in the reality that it was never a centralized, unitary religion to begin with. Much like building a single roof over a field full of tents, Hinduism came to be by applying one label to a collection of related but independent stories, beliefs, and practices. The common thread that weaves through the many aspects of this complex and multidimensional religion is what Hindus call *sanatana dharma*, which translates as "eternal tradition." To Hinduism's true believers, the Hindu faith has existed throughout the course of time and will continue to do so long into the future.

ESSENTIAL FACTS

DATE FOUNDED

There is no known date for the founding of Hinduism. The Vedic texts that define many Hindu beliefs and practices are believed to have been written in the Indian subcontinent between 1500 BCE and 300 BCE.

BASIC BELIEFS

Hinduism is both monotheistic and polytheistic in nature. Hindus believe in a Supreme Being known as Brahman, as well as multiple deity figures who are manifestations of Brahman. A belief in reincarnation and karma underscores many aspects of life. Hindus aim to escape the cyclical nature of life through moksha, the spiritual union with Brahman. The principle of dharma, through which Hindus strive to uphold moral law and perform the duties of their caste, is very important.

IMPORTANT HOLIDAYS AND EVENTS

- Diwali, the fall festival of lights
- Navratri, the celebration of the goddess Devi
- Holi, the spring festival of colors
- Maha Shivaratri, the solemn commemoration of Shiva

FAITH LEADERS

- Ram Mohan Roy discouraged idol worship and emphasized rationalism over revelation.

- Dayananda Sarasvati asserted that the Vedas were the only holy writings for Hindus, and he denounced practices such as discrimination by caste, child marriage, and the mistreatment of women.

- Paramahamsa Ramakrishna focused on mysticism as a way to unite with the divine presence, and he believed all religions worshipped the same God.

- Vivekananda believed the divine presence could be found in every person and every religion. He initiated many philanthropic enterprises that are still operating today.

- Mohandas Gandhi advocated nonviolent opposition to social injustice and was instrumental in helping India secure its independence from the United Kingdom.

NUMBER OF PEOPLE WHO PRACTICE HINDUISM

Approximately one billion people, or 15 percent of the world's population, identify as Hindus.

QUOTE

"In Hinduism, polytheism and monotheism coexist in a relationship much like the parts of a wheel. The many deities are like the spokes, all of which emanate from the hub and each playing an important role."

—*Ramdas Lamb, professor of religion, University of Hawaii*

GLOSSARY

ADHERENT

A person who practices a given religion or follows the teachings of a spiritual leader.

AVATAR

A Hindu deity's human form.

CONTEMPLATION

A mental state of praying or meditating, usually related to worship.

DEITY

A god or goddess.

DEVOTEE

A person who is a strong supporter of a religion or another cause.

DIASPORA

The movement of a people group away from their traditional homeland.

DOCTRINE

What is taught; teachings.

FERTILITY

Having to do with being able to reproduce.

ICON

A symbol or other representation that has special meaning to certain people; for example, a statue of a Hindu god.

LORE

Customs, beliefs, and stories traditional to a group or a place.

MANIFESTATION

A visible portrayal of something intangible.

MANTRA

A word or sound that is voiced repetitively during meditation to promote concentration.

MYSTICAL

Having to do with spiritual things that cannot be experienced with physical senses or thought.

NOMADIC

Moving from one place to another.

ORNATE

Decorated or built in a luxurious, highly adorned manner.

PANTHEON

The full array of a given thing; all the gods of a given religion.

PYRE

A pile of burnable material, especially one for burning a body as part of a funeral ceremony.

REINCARNATION

The process of being reborn in a different body.

REVELATION

Some truth related to God or a god that has been shown to people.

SECT

A group within a larger religion that holds distinct beliefs from others in that religion.

SECULAR

Nonreligious.

UNITARY

Being indivisible and whole; having only one nature.

UNIVERSALIST

Having to do with a belief that people in any religion or in no religion at all can know God.

YOGI

Someone who teaches yoga.

ADDITIONAL RESOURCES

SELECTED BIBLIOGRAPHY

Brodd, Jeffrey, et al. *Invitation to World Religions*. New York: Oxford UP, 2016. Print.

Esposito, John L., et al. *World Religions Today*. New York: Oxford UP, 2015. Print.

Flood, Gavin. *An Introduction to Hinduism*. New York: Cambridge UP, 1996. Print.

Knott, Kim. *Hinduism: A Very Short Introduction*. Oxford, United Kingdom: Oxford UP, 2016. Print.

FURTHER READINGS

McFarlane, Marilyn. *Sacred Stories: Wisdom from World Religions*. New York: Aladdin, 2012. Print.

Quinn, Jason. *Gandhi: My Life Is My Message*. New Delhi, India: Campfire, 2013. Print.

Rowell, Rebecca. *Ancient India*. Minneapolis, MN: Abdo, 2015. Print.

ONLINE RESOURCES

Booklinks
NONFICTION NETWORK
FREE! ONLINE NONFICTION RESOURCES

To learn more about Hinduism, visit **abdobooklinks.com**. These links are routinely monitored and updated to provide the most current information available.

MORE INFORMATION

For more information on this subject, contact or visit the following organizations:

PALACE OF GOLD

3759 McCrearys Ridge Rd.
Moundsville, WV 26041
304-843-1600 ext. 0
palaceofgold.com

Visitors are invited to tour the palace and grounds, which are modeled after those of an Indian kingdom. The palace is overseen by devotees of Krishna.

THE RUBIN MUSEUM OF ART

150 W. 17th St.
New York, NY 10011
212-620-5000
rubinmuseum.org

The Rubin Museum of Art features exhibitions and programs that foster awareness about the art and culture of the Himalayan region.

SOURCE NOTES

Chapter 1. Festival of Colors

1. Herb Scribner. "Does Utah Really Host the World's Largest Holi Festival?" *Deseret News*. Deseret News, 15 Mar. 2017. Web. 12 Feb. 2018.

2. Dominic Valente. "20th Holi Festival of Colors Draws Thousands to Spanish Fork." *Daily Herald*. Herald Communications, 28 Mar. 2016. Web. 12 Feb. 2018.

3. Peggy Fletcher Stack. "Utah Hindu Fest Passes the Mormon Test with Flying Colors." *Salt Lake Tribune*. Salt Lake Tribune, 27 Mar. 2014. Web. 12 Feb. 2018.

4. Herb Scribner. "Does Utah Really Host . . .?"

5. Ramdas Lamb. "Polytheism and Monotheism: A Hindu Perspective." *Huffington Post*. Huffington Post, 31 May 2011. Web. 12 Feb. 2018.

6. "The Global Religious Landscape: Hindus." *Pew Research Center*. Pew Research Center, 18 Dec. 2012. Web. 12 Feb. 2018.

7. Conrad Hackett. "By 2050, India to Have World's Largest Populations of Hindus and Muslims." *Pew Research Center: FacTank*. Pew Research Center, 21 Apr. 2015. Web. 12 Feb. 2018.

8. "India: 2015 Report on International Religious Freedom." *US Department of State*. US Department of State, 10 Aug. 2016. Web. 12 Feb. 2018.

9. Conrad Hackett. "By 2050, India to Have . . ."

10. "The World Factbook: Religions." *Central Intelligence Agency*. Central Intelligence Agency, n.d. Web. 12 Feb. 2018.

11. Van Buitenen, J. A. B., et al. "Hinduism." *Encyclopædia Britannica*. Encyclopædia Britannica, 25 Jan. 2017. Web. 12 Feb. 2018.

Chapter 2. Origins of Hinduism

1. Amrutur V. Srinivasan. *Hinduism for Dummies*. Hoboken, NJ: Wiley, 2011. Print. 20.

2. "Indian Village Where People Speak in Sanskrit." *BBC News*. BBC, 22 Dec. 2014. Web. 12 Feb. 2018.

3. Philip Goldberg. *American Veda: From Emerson and the Beatles to Yoga and Meditation: How Indian Spirituality Changed the West*. New York: Harmony, 2010. 39. Google Books. Web. 12 Feb. 2018.

4. Goldberg, Philip. *American Veda*. 144.

5. Jeffrey Brodd, et al. *Invitation to World Religions*. 2nd ed. New York: Oxford UP, 2016. Print. 103.

6. "What Is India's Caste System?" *BBC News*. BBC. 20 July 2017. Web. 12 Feb. 2018.

Chapter 3. Evolution and Colonialism

1. William Dalrymple. "The East India Company: The Original Corporate Raiders." *Guardian*. Guardian, 4 Mar. 2015. Web. 12 Feb. 2018.

Chapter 4. One God, Many, or None?

1. M. K. Gandhi. "Truth Is God." *MKGandhi.org*. Bombay Sarvoday Mandal and Gandhi Research Foundation, Jalgaon, n.d. Web. 12 Feb. 2018.

2. Jeffrey Brodd, et al. *Invitation to World Religions*. 2nd ed. New York: Oxford UP, 2016. Print. 93.

3. "Avatar: Hinduism." *Encyclopædia Britannica*. Encyclopædia Britannica, 2018. Web. 12 Feb. 2018.

4. Nida Najar and Suhasini Raj. "Indian State Is Expanding Penalty for Killing a Cow to Life in Prison." *New York Times*. New York Times, 31 Mar. 2017. Web. 12 Feb. 2018.

5. Petra Sorge. "India Cracks Down on Slaughter of Sacred Cows." *USA Today*. USA Today, 30 Dec. 2016. Web. 12 Feb. 2018.

SOURCE NOTES CONTINUED

Chapter 5. Key Concepts and Customs

1. Jeffrey Brodd, et al. *Invitation to World Religions*. 2nd ed. New York: Oxford UP, 2016. Print. 127.

Chapter 6. Reforming Hinduism

1. "Full Text of Swami Vivekananda's Chicago Speech of 1893." *Business Standard*. Business Standard, 11 Sept. 2017. Web. 12 Feb. 2018.

2. Dhananjay Keer. *Dr. Ambedkar: Life and Mission*. Mumbai: Popular Prakashan, 1990. 227. Google Books. Web. 12 Feb. 2018.

3. Kim Knott. *Hinduism: A Very Short Introduction*. Oxford: Oxford UP, 2016. Print. 82.

Chapter 7. Personal Devotion

1. Margot Adler. "To Some Hindus, Modern Yoga Has Lost Its Way." *MPR News*. NPR, 11 Apr. 2012. Web. 12 Feb. 2018.

2. Margot Adler. "To Some Hindus . . ."

3. Priyanka Boghani. "Maha Kumbh Mela Saw Record 120 Million Devotees." *PRI*. PRI, 11 Mar. 2013. Web. 12 Feb. 2018.

Chapter 8. Festivals and Holidays

1. Ritu Sharma. "As India's Rivers Turn Toxic, Religion Plays a Part." *UCANews*. UCANews.com, 19 Jan. 2014. Web. 12 Feb. 2018.

Chapter 9. Challenges

1. A. R. "Indian Reservations." *Economist*. Economist, 29 Jun. 2013. Web. 12 Feb. 2018.

2. Bhopinder Singh. "Much More Than the First Dalit President of India." *Tribune*. Tribune, 1 Jul. 2017. Web. 12 Feb. 2018.

3. Max Pearlstein. "Social Reform and the Caste System." *Brandeis NOW*. Brandeis University, 24 Apr. 2017. Web. 12 Feb. 2018.

4. Julie McCarthy. "The Caste Formerly Known as 'Untouchables' Demands a New Role in India." *MPR News*. NPR, 13 Aug. 2016. Web. 12 Feb. 2018.

5. "India: 2015 Report on International Religious Freedom." *US Department of State*. US Department of State, 10 Aug. 2016. Web. 12 Feb. 2018.

6. "BJP's Proposal Passed: Surya Namaskar Must in BMC-Run Schools." *India Express*. Indian Express, 24 Aug. 2016. Web. 12 Feb. 2018.

7. "India: 2015 Report . . ."

8. Kim Knott. *Hinduism: A Very Short Introduction*. Oxford: Oxford UP, 2016. Print. 79.

Chapter 10. Hinduism Present and Future

1. John L. Esposito, Darrell J. Fasching, and Todd T. Lewis. *World Religions Today*. New York: Oxford UP, 2015. Print. 299.

2. Kim Knott. *Hinduism: A Very Short Introduction*. Oxford: Oxford UP, 2016. Print. 93.

3. Brenda Goodman. "In a Suburb of Atlanta, a Temple Stops Traffic." *New York Times*. New York Times, 5 July 2007. Web. 12 Feb. 2018.

4. "$150 Million Akshardham Temple Coming Up in New Jersey." *American Bazaar*. American Bazaar, 21 July 2014. Web. 12 Feb. 2018.

5. "10 Most Famous Hindu Temples in America." *World Hindu News*. World Hindu News, 23 Apr. 2017. Web. 12 Feb. 2018.

6. Kathy Lohr. "Gleaming Hindu Temple to Open in Atlanta Suburb." *MPR News*. NPR, 15 Aug. 2007. Web. 12 Feb. 2018.

7. "Visitor Info: Things to Do & See." *BAPS Swaminarayan Sanstha: Shri Swaminarayan Mandir, Atlanta, GA, USA*. Bochasanwasi Shri Akshar Purushottam Swaminarayan Sanstha, 2017. Web. 12 Feb. 2018.

8. Van Buitenen, J. A. B., et al. "Hinduism." *Encyclopædia Britannica*. Encyclopædia Britannica, 25 Jan. 2017. Web. 12 Feb. 2018.

INDEX

ABOUT THE AUTHOR

Susan Bradley is an author, editor, fact-checker, and proofreader. She raised her family in Eagan, Minnesota, and lives there with her husband and dog.